The

Story by Jenny Giles

Illustrated by Isabel Lowe

It had been raining for a week.
Sam and his dog Spot
looked out of the window.

"Mom! Dad!" called Sam.
"Come and look at the water!
I can't see the garden!"

3

Rachel ran outside.
"Look at our car!" she said.
"It's in the water!"

"Oh, no!" said Dad, and he ran
   outside onto the steps.
"The river is coming up fast,"
   he said. "It's a flood."

"The water is going to come into the house!" said Mom. "Come on, all of you. Help me get everything out of the downstairs playroom."

Sam and Rachel ran to save their toys.

Then the muddy brown water came in.

It ran everywhere.

Everyone was safe upstairs, but . . .

"We can't get out!" said Rachel.

"No one can have a drink of water," said Dad. "It isn't clean."

"And the phone is dead," said Mom.

Then Spot barked and barked.
Sam said, "Look over there!
Spot has seen a boat."

They all waved, and the boat came
putt-putt-putting up to the steps.
"It's Andy McDonald," said Dad.
"Thanks for coming, Andy."

"You can't stay here," said Andy.
"Get your things and come
to our place."

They all climbed into the boat
and went slowly away
past the treetops.
Rachel looked back at the house.

"In a day or two
the river will go down," said Mom,
"And then we can come back . . ."

". . . and **clean up**," said Dad.